Computer Hacking

The Crash Course Guide to Learning Computer Hacking Fast & How to Hack for Beginners

Table Of Contents

Introduction

I want to thank you and congratulate you for downloading the book Computer Hacking: The Crash Course Guide to Learning Computer Hacking Fast & How to Hack For Beginners.

This book contains proven steps and strategies on how to become a truly experienced hacker, able to protect yourself from the danger lurking around online.

Here's an inescapable fact: you will need to know how hackers think in order to keep yourself fully protected from being hacked yourself.

If you do not develop your hacking skills then you will be susceptible to a variety of cyber-attacks yourself. In the age of the internet, nearly every piece of a person's life is digital. This means that the risk of cyber-attacks can affect your day to day life. By taking your time and learning about the world of hacking, you will be able to avoid dire consequences which you will face when being hacked.

It's time for you to become an amazing ethical hacker in order to keep you and your information protected. The more you are able to find out about this process, the easier you will find it to spot problems with your computer systems caused by hacking. By taking advantage of the information located in this eBook, you can heighten the amount of cyber knowledge you have. In the fast paced and technologically advanced world of today, having every advantage you can will allow you to succeed. Any business owner worth their salt needs to understand the particulars of hacking and how exactly it can help them secure their network and protect their sensitive information. In this book you will learn a lot of invaluable information which will help you significantly as a business owner in the 21st century.

So sit back and enjoy the information laid out in this book and ask yourself the question, what would you do if you were hacked tomorrow? Would you have a contingency plan or would it wipe you out? What are going to do about the danger posed by the hacking community? Are you ready to take on the hackers head on?

Chapter 1: Laying the Groundwork and Learning the Terminology

One of the hardest jobs a person can take on is as a business owner. There are so many different things you have to worry about when owning your own company. In the modern age, many companies utilize the power of the internet for their business. This means that in most cases, a company will have a computer network set up in their building. Most people are familiar with the term hacker, but often misinterpret its meaning and fail to realize the different types of hackers. In order to know the risk and dangers lurking around on your computer network, you will need to develop the mindset of a hacker. By creating a foundation of hacker knowledge, you will be able to spot problems on the network you have.

With all of the sensitive information most people have on their network, being hacked can compromise their livelihood and the livelihood of their customers. The last thing any business owner wants is to have their company look untrustworthy or unsafe in the eyes of the public. By arming yourself with as much information as you can about hacking, you will be able to get an idea of how these individuals think and how you can protect your network by implementing a number of different safeguards. The more tech savvy you are in this area of computing, the better off you and your company will ultimately be.

Knowing the Terminology and Lingo

The first thing you have to learn when trying to get into the mind of a hacker is the terminology and lingo used in the community. The work hacker is a blanket term that does not actually encompass all of the different factions contained within the community. Here are a few of the terms you need to become familiar with before proceeding.

- **External Hacker-**An external hacker is one of the most malicious and harmful of all of the terms you will learn. The main goal of an external hacker is to access all of the sensitive information on a computer system in order to use them for nefarious purposes. In most cases, these types of hackers are not particular about the type of companies or systems they attack. Most of the hackers out there view the sites and companies they hack as trophies. This means that the bigger the hack, the more of a reputation they get within their community.

- **Internal or Inside Hacker-** An internal or inside hacker is an individual who works for the company or site that tries to hack in from the inside. These types of hackers are among the most dangerous and usually go undetected for quite some time. The information that most inside hackers will obtain can be sold on the black market for a pretty penny. Many of the most damaging hacks in history have been pulled off from the inside, which is why it is so important for a business owner to find out about warning signs of an inside hack.

- **The Ethical Hacker-** The ethical hackers are the good guys in the world of hacking. In most cases, the ethical hacker is a business owner looking to gain knowledge of their own system and the trap doors that can be used against them. By learning to be an ethical hacker, you will be able to put up things to protect your network from intrusion and damage by external or internal sources.

Auditing and Ethical Hacking Are Not the Same Thing

One of the biggest misconceptions most business owners labor under is that auditing their network is the same thing as ethical hacking. The process of auditing is usually done by using different risk based tools, which is only done to verify there are security measures in place to protect from a certain type of attack. In basic terms, the only thing a business does during a security audit is to run down a checklist of dangers they perceive are out there and not actually what is going on. Even if you get a security expert to help with your audit, it still will not be nearly as efficient as ethical hacking.

When employing the technique of ethical hacking on your business network, you will be able view the various holes in your system that can cause trouble. The ethical hacking will not only check what you have in place on your network, but what you don't that will allow internal or external hackers to gain access to your sensitive information. The only issue most business owners have with ethical hacking is the lack of structure it has. Although performing this type of hacking is a bit unorganized, it can turn up much more information regarding issues you need to address with your system than a security audit will.

Have Your Ethical Hacking Policy Laid Out

Another foundational part of your ethical hacking is the policies you lay out for your business. You need to make sure you have a detailed breakdown of the practices you use to hack your own system. The document should layout the parts of the system that are hacked and how often it is done. This will allow you to inform new and old employees about the practices and measures you take to secure the system. In most cases, having a document like this will allow you to deter any internal hacking that may take place. If you have a certain date you do your ethical hacking on, be sure to let the managers know. Due to the interruption some of the hacking techniques may cause, keeping everyone in the loop will reduce confusion.

Why do You Need to Hack Your Computer System?

Most business owners have a hard time wrapping their mind around why they need to hack their own system. They figure they were the ones who helped set it up, so why do they need to break into it? In order to catch a hacker, you have to be able to think like they do. Each day, more and more people get into the hacking game, which only increases the risk you have of your system being infiltrated. By leaving your system weak and vulnerable, you will only be creating more stress and worry for yourself in the future. The practice of ethical hacking is known for the benefits it can bring to securing a network and keeping it out the reach of would be cyber-criminals.

Consistency is the Key

Once you have decided to implement the practice of ethical hacking, you need to think about the consistency at which you perform it. An external hacker is always working to hone their skills and learn more and more about how to hack into secured systems. By performing hacking on your own system on a regular basis, you will be able to get the kinks worked out of your system and avoid attacks. By failing to do your hacking on a regular basis, you will be putting your system at risk. By being able to anticipate the problems within your system and fixing them, you will be able to stay ahead of the game.

The Dangers of Infrastructure Attacks

One of the most common attacks a business is susceptible to is in regards to their network infrastructure. Most hackers will attack this part of your network first due to the accessibility factor is has. For the most part, a business network is accessible from just about anywhere, which is why hackers choose to attack it. Here are a few examples of the most common infrastructure attacks.

- **Exploiting Unsecured Portals-** One of the first attacks you need to be aware of regarding your network infrastructure is the exploitation of unsecured portals. If your network is not secured with a password, it is very easy for a hacker to gain access and run amuck in your system.

- **Network Protocol Weaknesses**- Another very common infrastructure attack has to do with the compromising of network protocols. In attacks like this, the hacker will bombard your system with various requests. The more requests the system has to deal with, the higher the chance of the system being knocked off line.

- **Spyware Concerns**- Among the most harmful hacks your system can undergo is the installation of spyware. This spyware will allow the hackers to view every piece of information that comes across the network. This information will allow the hackers to compromise the sensitive information you try so hard to keep safe.

Be Sure to Respect Privacy of Your Employees

When doing the ethical hacking of your system, you need to make sure you respect the privacy of the employees you have. While performing this process, you may come across personal information about the employees you have. If this information is not relevant to your business system security, then you need to leave it alone. The last thing you want to do is compromise the trust you have with your employees by snooping.

Once you have laid the foundation of your ethical hacking, you need to start thinking about the plan of attack and what you need to use to get the information. There are a number of tools out there that will allow you to analyze your system and find the holes that may exist. The time and effort you put into this process is more than worth it in the end. You can now move on to the second chapter where we will discuss tools to use, developing your process, and the profile of a malicious hacker.

Chapter 2: Establishing the Particulars of Your Ethical Hack

Now that you have established the need and purpose for your ethical hacking, you will need to start thinking about the particulars of this process. The last thing you want to do is go into this process without a clear idea of what you are doing due to the large room for error that exists. At first, you will need to start small with your hacks until you are able to learn a bit more about the process and how to work it to your advantage. By biting off more than you can chew to begin with, you may damage your system in the process. As time goes by you need to be prepared to launch a full scale attack of your system.

You need to consider the fact that would be hackers are not going to respect any part of your system, which can leave the scope of damage quite large. If you try and hold back during these ethical hacks, you will only be putting yourself at risk of attack. The more you can think like the hacker during this process, the better off you will be in the long run. The more time and effort you spend developing your plan of attack, the better you will be able to make sure your system is fully protected against hacker attacks. Make sure to do your homework on how to lay out your attack before you even begin, in order to reduce the amount of error you have. You need to view this process as a walk rather than a sprint. Taking your time and doing it right will allow you to do the job right and avoid errors that can cripple your system due to negligence or inexperience on your part.

What You Need to Consider

Now that you have started learning more about this process and what you will be able to accomplish with it, you will need to start thinking about the considerations that need to be made. The following are a few things you have to consider when trying to perform your ethical hacking:

- **Do You Want to Be Detected-** The first thing to think about is whether or not you want to be detected during your ethical hack? The more employees you tell about your hacking, the less effective it will be. If you have a lot of remote users of your system, you need to leave them out of the loop. The testing of the remote users on your system will give you a fair assessment of where your biggest holes are. Once you have decided whether you want to be detected and who you want to keep out of the loop, it will become easier to plan out your hack.

- **Getting a Basic Understanding of Systems Tested-** The next thing you need to consider when trying to ethically hack is the understanding you have of the systems you are going into. Although you do not have to have extensive knowledge of each system, you will need to get a basic idea of how they operate. This knowledge will allow you to avoid making costly mistakes and it will be easier for you to interpret the data you get. Without this knowledge you will also be at risk of not being able to understand what you are doing and how it is related to your business.

- **What To Do Once Vulnerabilities are Found-** When you are hacking your system, you will need to have a contingency plan on what you will do once problems have been discovered. If you start noticing inconsistencies with your system, then you need to follow the lead until you get an answer on what needs to be done to fix it.

The Steps to Follow During the Hack

Once you have figured out what the variables of your hack will be, you will be ready to start initializing the steps of the actual process. There is a certain roadmap you will need to follow in order to get the results you are looking for such as:

- **Follow the Path of a Hacker-** The first thing you need to do when trying to perform this hack is to follow the path of a hacker. A hacker will usually search for a business on Google, which can provide your business name and IP address to them. By having this type of information, you will be able to access the business via the network infrastructure. Once you have found your business and IP address on the internet, you will then need to hack into the server.

- **Focusing Your Efforts-** Once you have gotten in to your system, it will be time to narrow down which systems you will be going after. The more focused you can make your attacks, the more you will be able to find out about your system. Neglecting to have this type of focus, you run the risk not getting the information you need about your system.

- **Making Split Decisions-** There will inevitably be parts of your ethical hack that will take you go off in different directions. You will need to learn how to discern between good leads and those that will just send you off on a wild goose chase. The time and effort you spend learning this skill will save you a lot of trouble in the long run. The last thing you want to do during this hack is to chase leads that will only turn up nothing due to time and effort it will cost you.

- **Have a Plan To Fix The Holes-** The next thing you want to make sure of when trying to have a successful hack is to know what to do when you find holes in your system. All of the work you do will be negated without fixing the problems you have found. The more you re able to figure about where your system is vulnerable and what you can do about it, the better off you will be in the long run.

What Type of Tools Do You Need For the Job?

Another very important thing you have to consider when trying to get the right results for your hack is what type of tools you will use during your hacking. The right tools will make all of the difference and are a vital part of achieving success during this process. Here are a few of the tools you need to consider using when trying to ethically hack into your own system.

- **Getting around Passwords-** One of the first tools you need to find is a password cracker. You will have a number of passwords all over your system and without the right cracker, you will need a tool that can help you out. Without having this at your disposal, you run the risk of not being able to get the job done right. There are a number of different tools out there that can help you accomplish your password cracking. Simply search for 'password cracker' and you will find plenty of free software.

- **The Right Analysis Tools-** Once you have hacked into your system, you will need a tool that is able to analyze the information you are finding. There is software out there that will take the code on your site and allow you to find the holes in it. This type of software can be invaluable during this process and can allow you to detect things the naked eye would overlook. By taking the time and finding the right tools for this job, you will be able to get a comprehensive look at your system and what needs to be done to secure it better.

With all of the right tools and knowledge, you will be able to get into your system and check around to see what you notice. The more you can find out about your system and the holes in it, the better equipped you will be to keep your system in the right condition.

In order to do a complete and successful hack of your system, you will need to put yourself in the mindset of a hacker. In the next chapter, you will find out about hackers, how they choose their targets and the motivation they have for doing what they do. By having this information, you will better equipped to plan out of your ethical hack.

Chapter 3: Getting Inside the Mind of a Hacker

For the most part, people are largely uninformed when it comes to what a hacker is and what their main goals are for doing what they do. Most hackers out there today agree that they are misunderstood and largely misrepresented when it comes to how they are portrayed in the media as a whole. Before you begin to delve into the mindset of a hacker, you will need to comprehend what it is they are actually looking for. The more you are able to find out about what they are looking for in relation to holes in a website or network, the easier you will find it to get the right result from your efforts.

Why is Hacking Happening on Such a Frequent Basis These Days?

One of the first questions most business owners and individuals have is why does hacking happen so much these days? There are a number of different factors that have contributed to this, such as:

- **More Use of Networks and The Internet-** One of the biggest reasons for the increased hacking you hear about these days is the increased use of internet and network connectivity. The more access a hacker has to a business, through network portals, the easier it is for them. There are very few businesses out there that do not do a good bit of their business online, which is part of the increased risk. With more and more businesses going online, this hacking trend will not be stopping anytime soon.

- **Higher Degree of Anonymity-** Another reason for this increased hacking presence is the anonymity these individuals are allowed online. Most hackers are able to change their IP addresses. This higher level of anonymity is one of the reasons why most hackers seem so fearless due to the fact they think they cannot be caught. This can be done simply by using a proxy server website. You can also install simple plugins such as 'anonymox' for Mozilla Firefox.

- **More Hacking Tools on the Market-** Yet another advantage that a hacker has that allows them to get into your website is the overwhelming amount of tools on the market today. There are tons of different tools out there, from password crackers to maskers, which allow hackers to roam freely without fear of being discovered.

- **Wider Array of Coder Databases-** One of the top ways a hacker will get into a site is by using mistakes or holes in the code. There are hundreds if not thousands of lines of code out there and knowing how to manipulate them will allow you access. There are a large number of coder databases on the web that make it easy for would be hackers to reference the things they want to do before doing them. This helps to eliminate a good bit of the risk involved in the hacking of websites.

- **The Computerized Generation-** Another reason for the increased number of hackers out there is the access to computers children get at a young age. The more a child growing up can learn about computers, the easier it will be for them to do things like this simply. With more and more schools implementing the use of computers over text books, this trend has no signs of stopping any time soon.

The Skill Levels of Hackers in the Industry

Once you have seen why these attacks happen, you will need to learn about the various skill levels in the hacker industry. By knowing this type of information, you will be better equipped to handle the attacks you may be susceptible to. Here are a few of the different levels of hacking and what they involve.

- **The Script Kiddies-** One of the most common types of hackers out there are referred to as Script Kiddies. This is the lowest level of hacker out there and the skill level they have is very minimal. These types of hackers will usually only know how to use the various online hacking tools and will have no real knowledge of the process. In most cases, the attacks these type of hackers can do is very minimal and can be reversed with little effort.

- **The Criminal Hackers-** Another more dangerous type of hacker is the criminal variety, which only hacks for personal gain. In most cases, these types of hackers are a part of a larger network of hackers. The damage you can get from these types of hackers can be quite substantial and can bring down the network you have. Most of the hackers in these networks have been in the game for years and have just enough experience to do real damage to your system.

- **The Security Researcher-** The security researcher is a different breed of hacker altogether. The only reason these hackers do what they do to help companies secure their networks from harmful attacks. In most cases, this variety of hacker is among the most highly trained out there. When it comes to finding holes in a systems or potential backdoors in a system, the security researcher is the person who can find it and tell you how to fix it.

Elements That Allow Hackers to Do What They Do

Most people out there have little to no idea why and how a hacker does what they do. There are a number of elements that work together that allow the hackers to do what they do. The following are a few of those elements and how they allow hackers to have access.

- **Poorly Managed Systems-** One of the main reasons why hackers are able to access so many networks is due to their poor management. Most of the computer systems out there have not been ethically hacked, which leaves them wide open for intrusion by a hacker. Usually, a network will not be monitored in smaller businesses, which will leave any attacks by hackers largely undetected.

- **Outdated Network Security-** With all of the updates and new network security products coming out on a weekly basis, trying to keep up with them all can be a bit of a chore for a network administrator. By neglecting to use the most current security solutions for a network, you are running the risk of being hacked by tech savvy individuals.

- **Slow and Steady Hacks-** Another very popular reason a hacker is able to do their job is the fact that by acting slowly, they can go largely undetected. By not having a person in charge of network intrusions, you are going to be susceptible to these types of slow hacks.

- **Trouble after Business Hours** Most business owners fail to realize that the majority of the hacking they will experience will be after hours. This makes the damage much worse due to the fact that it will be hours before you are made aware of the situation. The longer you have to wait to address issues, the more damage a hacker will be able to do on your system. By having a security alert system in place, you will be able to get alerts as soon as trouble is detected, which will allow you to act in a fast manner.

- **Heightened Complexity of Information Systems-** The next reason for the majority of most business hacks is the complexity of the information systems out there. These systems are hard for most business owners to navigate and understand, which is why they usually miss vital components that lead to hacks. If you are not sure about how to manage your information system, then you will need to consult with a professional to get some help. They will be able to give you the information needed to secure yourself and the information you have on your particular network.

Now that you have the understanding needed about the hackers and what they are capable of, you can delve into the various types of hacking out there and how they gain the information needed to penetrate networks. In the next chapter, you will discover how the practice of Social Engineering can allow you to gain the information you need to hack a network. There are a variety of different ways a hacker can use social engineering to their advantage, which makes it a vital skill for you to learn when trying hack.

Chapter 4: The Social Engineering Tool

As stated previously in this book, in order to get into the ethical hacking game, you first need to think like a hacker. There are a number of tricks and tools a hacker uses to gain access to the things they want. As an ethical hacker, you will have to learn how to use these tools for good rather than for nefarious purposes. Refusing to delve into the world of hackers and the tools they use will make your efforts pointless and will leave you susceptible to certain types of attacks. When trying to get into this world, you either have to go all the way or not at all.

With all of the tools and tricks a hacker has at their disposal, trying to pick the best one to mimic can be a bit hard. In most cases, you will have to run the gambit on the methods used in order to find the best fit for the type of things you are trying to do. By leaving your options open and learning as much as you can, you will be able to get better at ethically hacking your system. In this chapter, you will learn about social engineering and how it is used by hackers to get what they want.

Familiarizing Yourself with Social Engineering

For the most part, many people have never heard about social engineering, which is why it is such a widely used tool in the world of hacking. The malicious hackers out there use a process whereby they engage with people inside of a potential marked company in order to gain information they are not able to get on their own. The information they gain from these people is then used to gain access to the system and take it for all its worth. Other types of information gathering techniques, such as dumpster surfing or over the shoulder thefts are usually used with social engineering as part of a grand scheme to gain access. Here are a few of the most common types of social engineering performed by hackers.

- **Using the Support Personnel-** One of the most popular ways a hacker will use this technique is by contacting the support personnel of a particular company and making up a story to gain access. In most cases, the hacker will rig up a software update that has a hidden patch in it. When the support personnel installs it, this gives them the access they need to get the job done. The patch will allow the hacker remote access to the system, which gives them the 'in' they need to start the destruction of the internal workings of the infrastructure. This can often be done by calling up pretending to be from the tech department, and asking for the computers TeamViewer ID in order to do some quick maintenance.

- **Posing as Vendors-** Another very common tactic used by a hacker is posing as a vendor in need of passwords to update certain parts of the system. You would be surprised at how willing most support personnel are to give out this information without verifying anything. It only takes a little bit of sensitive information like this to leak out to allow the hackers the access they need to create mayhem on the site.

- **Good Ole Phishing-** Perhaps the oldest method of gaining access through the social engineering spectrum is phishing emails. These are generic emails sent out that are packed with viruses. Once these emails are open on the system, the hacker can start to figure out passwords. With these passwords, the hacker will have access to a variety of sensitive information. Make sure you let all employees know that emails from unknown entities should not be opened on the system due to the damage they can bring.

By knowing these methods, you will be able to prevent them from happening. The more security safeguards you can put in place to prevent things like this, the easier you will find it to avoid the negative consequences brought on by the success of these techniques.

Testing Your Staff for Susceptibility

Now that you know about how social engineering works, you will need to implement it as part of your ethical hacking. You want to be able to rest assured that your staff are not falling for these tricks and the only way to do that is by testing them. By posing as someone else, you will be able to see whether or not you can gain access to your own system by going through your staff. The lessons you learn doing this will allow you to increase your security and see where the holes in your support staff are. If you are unable to pose as someone else, then you can always hire a third party to do it for you. There are a number of businesses out there who can test your staff to see if social engineering can gain them access to your system. The money you pay a company like this will be well worth it in the end if you are able to secure your company the right way.

The Goldmine the Hackers Hope to Stumble Upon

The hackers who perform the techniques outlined above do this in order to gain access to certain information. There are a number of things a hacker will consider a goldmine if they are able to gain access to them. Here are a few of the items a hacker is looking for when trying to perform the social engineering cons.

- **Charts Laying out Business Structure-** If a hacker is able to get their hands on this type of chart, they can piece together the individuals they need to go after. By knowing the higher level members of a company, the hacker will be able to get a hit list in place for who to hack first.

- **Handbooks with Security Policies-** When trying to perform a successful hack, the hackers need to know the security measures you already have in place. By gaining access to an employee handbook, the hacker will be able to see what to avoid and what areas of your network are vulnerable.

- **Diagrams of Your Network-** The last thing you want is for a hacker to get their hands on this document. This will basically give them a road map to your system, which will make it much easier for them to tear it apart. Make sure you are very careful with these documents and that you only put them in the hands of individuals that need to have them.

- **Password Documentation-** Another very sensitive document you have to be very protective of is password documentation. In most cases, a business owner will have a list of the important passwords on their system and in the wrong hands this could be used for harm to your network. A hacker is most intrigued by this type of list due to the simplicity it will bring to the hack.

- **Sensitive Emails-** Among the most commonly used documents by a hacker are sensitive emails. In most cases, email accounts are easily hacked and can be used for a variety of different purposes for a hacker. You need to try to keep sensitive information off of emails as much as you can due to the danger it can cause you.

Spotting a Social Engineering Attempt

There are a number of ways you can spot an attempted social engineering hack if you know what to look for. The following are a few red flags to look for when trying to spot this hack:

- **Name Dropping for No Reason-**If you get a call from a person who immediately starts name dropping people who are high up in your company, then beware. In most cases, hackers will do this to establish familiarity with the mark and then exploit it.

- **Threats about Reprimands-** Another very common thing you may experience during this attempted hack is threats about reprimands if the needs of the hacker aren't met. Fear can be an effective tool when used right. If you are not sure of who the person is, you need to view these threats as false instead of becoming emotional or frightened by them.

- **Hesitance When Questioned-** In some cases, you may be able to spot this type of hack by questioning the caller or visitor. By challenging what they are telling you, it may be easier to spot hesitance within them. If the person is in your presence, be sure to look for odd behavior as a way to discern whether or not they might be hackers.

By staying vigilant and keeping your staff that way as well, you can avoid being scammed by a hacker. The time you put into preparing your staff for this type of hack will be well worth it. In some cases, it will be wise to attempt to hack your own employees to make sure they aren't vulnerable to this type of attack.

Now that you have found out about the social engineering hack, you are ready to move on in your hacking journey. In the next chapter, you will find out about physical vulnerabilities that may leave you open for attack.

Chapter 5: Hacks Using Physical Security Flaws

One of the biggest misconceptions most business owners have regarding hackers is that they only use the computer to do their job. While the main weapon of choice for a hacker is their computer, on occasion they will do some real world reconnaissance in order to gain more information about a potential mark. Most business owners fail to realize just how easy it is for a hacker to gain access to their building. In most cases, the physical security of a building is overlooked in order to focus more on the cyber-security. In order to make sure your building is secure, you will need to perform checks to ensure its safety.

While you need to avoid going to extremes, you want to test your building and the complexity involved with gaining access to it. By taking an outsiders prospective, you will be able to look at your security objectively and find out whether or not you make the grade. It is very easy for a hacker to get into your office and access your data by utilizing various social engineering tricks on your staff. Having a trustworthy appearance can help a hacker gain entrance easily and then let them wreak havoc in your office. The last thing you want to do is have your business opened up for these types of attacks. The time and effort you spend trying to secure your building will be more than worth it when you consider the damage a hacker can do from inside of your building. Just like ethically hacking a computer network, assessing your physical security will take some time and planning. The more you are able to find out about techniques used by real world hackers, the easier you will find it to check your business out from an objective standpoint.

Knowing Your Vulnerabilities

Now that you understand a bit about the process used by a hacker to take advantage of the physical vulnerabilities of a company, you can start to take a look at your own company. The following are a few of the most common vulnerabilities that a business will have that can be taken advantage of by a hacker.

- **Lack of a Front Desk Presence-** One of the most common vulnerabilities a company can have is the lack of a front desk receptionist. A receptionist can be a very valuable tool when trying to keep people from entering your business. The last thing you want to do is make it easy on the hacker to just walk into your business and take a look around.

- **No Sign In or Escort Needed-** When trying to keep the hackers out of your building, you will need to think about what you can do before they even get to your door. Most businesses do not have sign in sheets or escorts to walk visitors around with. This can create a problem and can make it very easy for would- be hackers to walk in and gain access to whatever they wanted. By putting a person at the front door of your business that requires ID and verification from visitors, you can significantly reduce the chances of being infiltrated by a hacker.

- **Trusting Employees-** For most hackers trying to enter a building, using vendor uniforms is a tactic commonly employed. In most cases, employees will not question someone in a uniform they recognize.

Having employees that are too trusting regarding vendors can cause a plethora of problems and can allow hackers the access they want for their mission.

- **Open Doors are Like Invitations-** Among the first things a hacker will look for in a potential target is the type of locks they have on their doors and the condition of them during the day. If your employees have a habit of leaving the doors in your office propped open during the day, then you are at a higher risk of hacker intrusion. You have to make sure your doors stay closed and that they are equipped with some of the most up to date locking systems on the market. One of the best types of systems to have is an access control. These systems use key cards, which are very hard to replicate. This will help to keep hackers out of your building and will allow you to keep your data and computers safe

- **Easily Accessible Computer Rooms-** One of the most potentially dangerous vulnerabilities you can have in your business is easily accessible computer rooms. If you have these rooms opened to the public, then it will be very easy for a hacker to come in and get the information they need to compromise your network. Ideally, you want to have your computers secured with locks and guards. This will allow you to keep your sensitive information out of the hands of hackers.

- **Unsecured Work Areas-** Another harmful vulnerability you can have in your business is unsecured work areas. By not having your work areas under lock and key, you will be allowing hackers to look over the shoulders of your workers. This can allow the hacker to gain sensitive information that will allow them the access they need to get into your system.

By knowing the type of things a hacker will look for, you are better equipped to start eliminating the risks you see around your office building. The more you are able to find out about the mindset of the hacker, the easier it will be for you to get exactly what you need in regards to additional security measures.

Utility Issues That Can Cause a Lot of Trouble

In some cases, the vulnerability you have in your office space will be caused by utility problems rather than the building design. By takings stock of every part of your building, you will be able to see where the holes are and what vulnerability has the potential to cripple your network in the wrong hands. Here are a few of the utility problems you may want to address due to the danger they pose.

- **The Condition of Your Power Protection Equipment**- Nearly any office that has a good bit of electronics will have power protection equipment. Having things like surge protectors is vital in keeping the electronics in your office safe and secure during bad weather. You need to assess the location of your surge protectors and decide whether or not it would be easy for a hacker to gain access to it. If easily accessible, the hacker can walk in and flip switches, starting all kinds of havoc. You have to make sure the surge protectors you have are out of sight and protected.

- **Know Your Security System**- Another very important thing you need to consider when trying to assess your utilities is what happens to your security system when the power goes off. The last thing you want is for the security system to open everything during an outage. Make sure you speak with the security company to get an idea of how you can stop this from happening. In some cases, getting an individual power back up for this system will be a great idea.

- **Assess Your Fire Security-** When trying to secure your building, you need to pay special attention to the fire protection you have in play. If there is a fire alarm system in your building, then you have to consider where the pulls are located. It would be easy for a hacker to pull one of these and set off your alarm. While all the chaos is going on, they will be able to gain access to your vital information. Be sure to speak with the company handling your fire alarm to get an idea of what can be done to reduce the chance of this happening.

- **Where are Your Data Wires?** – You need to also consider where the wires that run your computer network are, and whether or not they are easily accessible. The last thing you want is to have your data cables exposed to a hacker due to the damage they can do with them. By using tracking and other materials, you will be able to protect and mask the wires. The time you spend performing these types of security measures will be more than worth it.

Your Employees and Their Behavior

Another very important thing you have to consider when trying to secure your offices against intrusion by a hacker is the way your employees handle sensitive information. The last thing you want is to have sensitive documents just laying around without any type of covering on them. All a hacker would have to do in this case is walk by and snag these documents off of a cluttered desk. This means they would have the ammunition needed to get into your system and create mayhem. You need to make sure you have policies in place regarding the handling of sensitive documents in your work place. The more your employees know about this, the safer your place of business will be.

By taking the time to perform an assessment on your physical vulnerabilities, you will be able to make sure your business is as secure as possible. In the next chapter we will discuss how to get your team on board about your ethical hacking and why this method is the only way to find the holes in your system.

Chapter 6: The Importance of Team Involvement

Most business owners have the misconception that the team they have around them will just automatically support the ethical hacking they want to do. In most cases, this is not true due to their lack of understanding on the subject. In order to have any type of success with this process, you will have to get all hands on deck with the ethical hack. You will need to spend some time going over the particulars with your management so they understand what is going on. The last thing any business owner wants to do is jam something like this down the throats of their staff.

The only way you will be able to win over your staff is by educating the same way you were educated yourself. By addressing any concerns they have, you will be able to put their mind at ease and get them to understand the importance of what you are trying to do. Addressing them in a calm, cool and collected manner will allow you to get your point across much easier. By taking your time and plotting out what you are going to say, you will be able to achieve the success you want with this project.

Addressing Your Employees about Ethical Hacking

Once you are ready to talk with your staff about the ethical hacking you want to do, you will need to lay out a strategy on how you will address them and what you will say to get your point across. The last thing you need to do is go into a meeting with your staff unprepared due to the importance of the subject. The following are a few things you need to discuss with your employees to get them on your side regarding ethical hacking.

- **Reasons Why You Can't Be Hacked-** The first thing you need to relay to your staff is why it would be bad if you were hacked. You need to have a few examples of similar companies who have been hacked and how badly it affected them. By giving them a side by side type comparison, you will be able to open their eyes to what the real issues are.

- **The Loss of Intellectual Property-** The next thing you need to focus on when trying to find the right way to let your staff know about your ethical hacking is the intellectual property that will be exposed. By having your business intellectual property in the hands of a hacker, you run the risk of not being able to conduct business as usual any more. You want to inform your staff and not use fear tactics to get them over to your side.

- **Personal Information Exposed** — Another very important thing you need to let your staff know when talking about hacking is how their personal information can be exposed. The last thing anyone wants is to have their personal information in the hands of a cyber-criminal. In most cases, this will get you the response you want and get compliance from each of the employees on using ethical hacking.

The time and effort you put into this process will be more than worth it when you are able to perform tests on your network. With all of your crew on board with this process, you will be able to get the information you are in search of to keep your network safe and secured from hacks and other types of cyber-attacks.

Why Hacking is the Best Way to Test

As discussed earlier in the book, the only way to truly test your network is by hacking it yourself. There are a number of different reasons to use this process for your business such as:

- **Using Their Own Weapons against Them-** The major reason why using this technique is so successful is the fact you are using the tactics of a hacker against them. By reverse engineering the tips and tricks of the trade, you will be able to make sure your network is safe.

- **Staying Up to Date-** When using the ethical hacking method, you will be able to stay up to date on all of the tools on the market for hackers. This will allow you to avoid having them used on your network and can allow you to put a variety of safeguards in place. Keeping your head in the game and being aware of all of the tools being put to use in the hacker community is a great way to reduce the danger your business faces in cyberspace.

- **Security Checklists are Unsuccessful-** Some business owners argue that making security checklists to follow can do just as much good as an ethical hacker. This is not the case due to the lack of depth a security checklist has. A hacker will not stop when they hit one roadblock, which is why it is so important to put yourself in the hacker mindset.

- **Practice Can Make Perfect-** After you do your ethical hacking a few times, it will become second nature to find the holes in your network without having to do a lot of work. You will be able to detect anomalies with your system much faster by having safeguards in place. The faster you are able to stop a cyber-attack, the less damage you will have to worry about to your system.

Before you go off and try to do your own ethical hacking, keep these common mistakes in mind so you can avoid them during your hack:

- **Getting Every Hole Fixed-** One of the biggest misconceptions a business owner will have before an ethical hack is that they will catch all of the vulnerabilities in their system. In all actuality, it may take a while to catch all of the holes in your network. By being persistent, you will be able to get all of the holes sealed up in your system.

- **Lack of Consistency-** Another mistake most business owners make is only testing their system on occasion. The more consistent you are with this process, the easier it will be for you to keep your system safe and secure. You want to start an ethical hacking schedule so you can stay abreast of any changes you may encounter.

- **No Planning-** When trying to get the most out of your ethical hacking you will need to have a plan of attack. By having an idea of where you are going with the hack, you will be able to have much more success with the process as a whole.

- **Using Professionals When Needed-** You need to make sure you know your limitations when doing this hack. If you run into a problem and you do not know what to do, you need to call in a pro to help you out. Trying to do everything will usually end in you messing something up. The money you pay a professional for their services is more than worth it when you consider the negative consequences of not using them when needed.

By taking this information you have learned and using it for good, you will be able to have a safe and secure network to compute on. Making sure you have everyone in your business on the same page is a big part of being successful with this type of hacking. The time and effort you put into learning and preparing for an ethical hack will more than pay off in the end.

Conclusion

Thank you again for downloading this book!

I hope this book was able to help you to get a grasp on the world of hacking and how ethical hacking can benefit you and your business.

The next step is to put into action the knowledge you have gained from this book.

Finally, if you enjoyed this book, please take the time to share your thoughts and post a review on Amazon. It'd be greatly appreciated!

Thank you and good luck!

Book Description

Most people are quite familiar with the word hacker due to the attention these entities get in the media. In this book, you will learn about how the world of hacking is growing and what you can do to protect your business from being the victim of a hacking. The last thing any business owner wants to do is leave themselves open to attacks due to lack of knowledge and planning on their part. This book will show you how you can take control of the holes in your network. The more you are able to find out about the world of hacking and how you can use it to your advantage, the easier you will find it to keep your computer network safe.

In this book you will learn such things at:

- The common techniques used by a hacker to gain entrance into the network of their choice.

- How social engineering is used to gain and then betray the trust of employees and team members.

- Ways you can test your workers to see how susceptible you are to social engineering.

- Tests you can run on your network and hacks that can be helpful in gaining a load of information on holes to be fixed

- Putting yourself inside the mind of a hacker, which can allow you to look at your network objectively.

By learning to ethically hack your own system, you will be able to learn invaluable information that will allow you to secure the network you have.

www.ingramcontent.com/pod-product-compliance
Lightning Source LLC
Chambersburg PA
CBHW070904070326
40690CB00009B/1981